THE POWER OF PRAYERS

"And as he prayed, the fashion of his countenance was altered, and his raiment was white and glistering."

Luke 9:29

By
Franklin N. Abazie

The Power of Prayers

COPYRIGHT 2018 BY Franklin N Abazie
ISBN: 978-1-945-133-70-1
All right reserved. This book or any portion thereof may not be reproduced or used in any manner whatsoever without the express written permission of the publisher, except for the use of brief quotations in a book review. All Bible quotes are from King James Version and others as noted.

Published by: F N ABAZIE PUBLISHING HOUSE---
a.k.a,
Empowerment Bookstore:

That I may publish with the voice of thanksgiving and tell of all thy wondrous works. **Psalms26:7**

To order additional copies, wholesales or booking: Call the Church office (973-372-7518)
or Empowerment Bookstore Hotline 973-393-8518
Worship address:
343 Sanford Avenue Newark New Jersey 07106
Administrative Head Office address:
33 Schley Street Newark New Jersey 07112
Email:pastorfranknto@yahoo.com
Website www.fnabaziehealingministries.org
Publishing House: www.fnabaziepublishinghouse.org

This book is a production of F N Abazie Publishing House.

A publication Arms of Miracle of God Ministries 2018
First Edition

CONTENTS

THE MANDATE OF THE COMMISSION...........iv

ARMS OF THE COMMISSION............................v

INTRODUCTION...viii

CHAPTER 1

1. Prevailing Prayer 59

CHAPTER 2

2. Hindrances to Prayer..71

CHAPTER 3

3. Prayer of Salvation..110

CHAPTER 4

4. About the Author...119

THE MANDATE OF THE COMMISSION

"THE MOMENT IS DUE TO IMPACT YOUR WORLD THROUGH THE REVIVAL OF THE HEALING & MIRACLE MINISTRY OF JESUS CHRIST OF NAZARETH.

I AM SENDING YOU TO RESTORE HEALTH UNTO THEE AND I WILL HEAL THEE OF THY WOUNDS, SAID THE LORD OF HOST."

ARMS OF THE COMMISSION

1) F N Abazie Ministries-Miracle of God Ministries (Miracle Chapel Intl)

2) F N Abazie TV Ministries: Global Television Ministry Outreach.

3) F N Abazie Radio Ministries: Radio Broadcasting Outreach.

4) F N Abazie Publishing House: Book Publication.

5) F N Abazie Bible School: also called Word of Healing Bible School (W.O.H.B.S)

6) F N Abazie Evangelistic Ass: Miracle of God Ministries: Global Crusade

7) Empowerment Bookstore: Book distribution.

8) F N Abazie Helping Hands: Meeting the help of the needy world wide

9) F N Abazie Disaster Recovery Mission: Global Disaster Recovery.

10) F N Abazie Prison Ministry: Prison Ministry for all convicts "Second chance"

Some of our ministry arms are waiting the appointed time to commence

FAVOR CONFESSION

Father thank you for making me righteous and accepted through the blood of Jesus Christ. Because of that, I am blessed and highly favored by God. I am the subject of your affection. Your favor surrounds me as a shield, and the first thing that people see around me is your favored shield.

Thank you that I have favor with you and man today. All day long people go out of their way to bless me and help me. I have favor with everyone that I deal with today. Doors that were once closed are now opened for me. I receive preferential treatment, and I have special privileges, I am Gods favored child.

No good thing will he withhold from me. Because of Gods favor my enemies cannot triumph over my life. I have supernatural increase and promotion. I declare restoration to everything that the devil has stolen from my life. I have honor in the midst of my adversaries and an increase in assets, especially in real estate and expansion of territories.

Because I am highly favored by God, I experience great victories, supernatural turnarounds, and miraculous breakthrough in the midst of great impossibilities. I receive recognition, prominence, and honor. Petitions are granted to me even by ungodly authorities. Policies, rules, regulations, and laws are changed and reverse on my behalf.

I win battles that I don't even have to fight, because God fights them for me. This is the day, the set time and the designated moment for me to experience the free favor of God, that profusely and lavishly abound on my behalf in Jesus name. Amen.

INTRODUCTION

"And he spake a parable unto them to this end, that men ought always to pray, and not to faint."
Luke18:1

I greet you in the Name of Jesus Christ the son of the living God. I thank the Lord for this great chance to meet you here. Perhaps we will never meet in person but permit me to say, I am glad to meet you. I love prayer. I am a man of prayers. I believe strongly in the power of prayer. I believe my life is a product of prayers.

In this small book we will be examining the power of prevailing and intercessory prayers. If you have not formed the habit of prayer as a lifestyle by now. I will strongly encourage you to take your prayer life very serious.

We are told. *"Watch and pray, that ye enter not into temptation: the spirit indeed is willing, but the flesh is weak."*
Mathew26:41

Also in **Mark14:38**, *"Watch ye and pray, lest ye enter into temptation. The spirit truly is ready, but the flesh is weak."*

This small book of prayer has been written to encourage and inspire you to pray often. I believe we must incorporate prayers into our busy lifestyle.

Come with me as we both reveal what the Holy Ghost has been saying about the power of prayer.

Happy Reading!

HIS DESTINY WAS THE CROSS....

HIS PURPOSE WAS LOVE.....

HIS REASON WAS YOU....

"But thou, when thou prayest, enter into thy closet, and when thou hast shut thy door, pray to thy Father which is in secret; and thy Father which seeth in secret shall reward thee openly."

Mathew6:7

"Watch ye and pray, lest ye enter into temptation. The spirit truly is ready, but the flesh is weak."

Mark 14:38

"Watch and pray, that ye enter not into temptation: the spirit indeed is willing, but the flesh is weak."

Mathew26:41

Prayer Points

"If ye shall ask any thing in my name, I will do it.." **John 14:14**

Holy Spirit of God frustrate and disappoint, every one that is against my life and family, in the name of Jesus.

Father Lord destroy every demonic networks and traps against my progress in life in the name of Jesus.

Fire of God, destroy every demonic projection and curses against my life and destiny in the name of Jesus.

Every spell and curses pronounced against my destiny, break, in the name of Jesus.

Hand of God cage every power militating against my rising in life, in the name of Jesus.

Power of God silent every voice raising a counter motion against my elevation, in the mighty name of Jesus.

Blood of Jesus neutralize every spirit of Balaam hired to hinder my life, ministry, and career, the name of Jesus.

Fire of God destroy every curse that I have brought into my life through ignorance and disobedience, break by fire, in the name of Jesus.

Ancient of day destroy every power harassing my ministry in the name of Jesus.

Father God deliver me from invincible forces militating against my life and destiny.

Power of God frustrate every coven and demonic network, designed to frustrate and hinder my success in life, in the name of Jesus.

I dismantle every strong hold designed to imprison my talent in the mighty name of Jesus.

I reject every cycle of frustration, in the name of Jesus.

Power of God paralyze every agent assigned to frustrate my life in the name of Jesus.

Finger of God, grant me supernatural speed against all my contenders in the name of Jesus.

By the blood of Jesus, I destroy every familiar spirit caging my life and career.

Fire of God arrest every demonic agents, assigned to police my destiny and marriage.

By the blood of Jesus, I proclaim no weapon fashioned against me shall ever prosper.

Holy Spirit of God break me through and forward in life in the mighty name of Jesus.

God, smash me and renew my strength, in the name of Jesus.

Holy Spirit, open my eyes to see beyond the visible to the invisible, in the name of Jesus.

Father Lord grant me strength and power in the name of Jesus.

O Lord, liberate my spirit to follow the leading of the Holy Spirit.

Holy Spirit, teach me to pray through problems instead of praying about, it in the name of Jesus.

Father Lord, deliver me from the false accusation in life, in the name of Jesus.

By the blood of Jesus, every evil spiritual padlock and evil chain hindering my success, be roasted, in the name of Jesus.

By the blood of Jesus I rebuke every spirit of spiritual deafness and blindness in my life, in the name of Jesus.

Father Lord, empower me to dominate the enemy of my destiny in the name of Jesus.

Jesus Christ of Nazareth, heal my infirmities in the name of Jesus.

Lord, anoint my eyes and my ears that they may see and hear wondrous things from heaven.

Father Lord, anoint me with power and authority to dominate all my enemies in the name of Jesus.

Fire of God roast every giant rising up against my life and career.

Holy Spirit of God destroy all my oppressors in the name of Jesus.

Angels of good new, bring my good news to me in the mighty name of Jesus.

Every strong man holding me down, lose your hold now in the name of Jesus.

I nullify every demonic prediction over my life in the name of Jesus.

By the blood of Jesus, I flush out every polluted deposit of the enemy in my life.

By the blood of Jesus, I paralyze every enemy of my promotion in the name of Jesus.

Father Lord, destroy any power tormenting my life that is not from you.

Holy Ghost fire, ignite the fire of revival in my life.

By the blood of Jesus, I declare victory over every conflicting trial.

By the Blood of Jesus, I command the arrest of every demonic spirit, militating against my life .

By the blood of Jesus, I proclaimed the blood of Jesus, over every device of the enemy.

By the blood of Jesus, I revoke stagnation and hardship over my life in the name of Jesus.

Holy Ghost fire, destroy every satanic arrangement in my life, in the name of Jesus.

It is written, *"do not be afraid of sudden terror; nor of the trouble from the wicked when it comes; for the Lord will be your confidence. And will keep your foot from being caught."* **(Proverb 3:26)**.

Therefore, O Lord, cover us and our loved ones from the activities of terrorists, in Jesus name!

It is written, *"avenge me of my adversary"* **(Luke. 18:3)**.

Therefore, O Lord, arise and avenge us of all my adversaries in the name of Jesus!

It is written, *"they fought from the heavens; the stars from their courses fought against Sisera."* **(Judges. 5:20)**.

Therefore O heavens, fight for us in Jesus name!

It is written, *"I will purge the rebels from among you, and those who transgress against me; I will bring them out of the country where they dwell, but they shall not enter the land of Israel. They will know that I am the Lord."* **(Ezekiel. 20:38)**

Therefore, O Lord, purge and sanitize our household in the name of Jesus!

It is written, *"then it was so, after all your wickedness – "woe, woe to you!" says the Lord God."* **(Ezekiel. 16:23)**

Therefore, woe unto all the vessels that the enemy is using to do us harm in the name of Jesus!

It is written, *"behold therefore, I stretch out my hand against you, admonished your allotment, and gave you up to the will of those who hate you..."* **(Ezekiel. 16:27)**

Therefore, let our enemies be delivered into the hands of their enemies in Jesus name!

It is written, *"you shall be for fuel of fire; your blood shall be in the midst of the land. You shall not be remembered, for I the Lord have spoken."* **(Ezekiel. 21:32)**

Therefore, let all our spiritual enemies become fuel for divine fire in Jesus name!

It is written, *"Then they will know that I am the Lord, when I have set a fire in Egypt and all her helpers are destroyed."* **(Ezekiel. 30:8)**.

Therefore, O Lord, let all the helpers of our enemies be destroyed in the name of Jesus.

It is written, *"and the people to whom they prophesy shall be cast out in the streets of Jerusalem because of the famine and the sword; they will have no one to bury them – them nor their wives, their sons nor their daughters – for I will pour their wickedness on them."* **(Jer. 14:16)**.

Therefore, O Lord, pour the wickedness of those who seek to destroy us upon their own heads in the name of Jesus!

It is written, *"Call together the archers against Babylon. All you who bend the bow encamp against it all around; let none of them escape. Repay her according to her work; According to all she has done, do to her; for she has been poured against the Lord, against the Holy one of Israel."* **(Jer. 50:29)**.

Therefore, let all the hosts of the Lord turn against our spiritual enemies in Jesus name!

It is written, *"let God arise, let His enemies be scattered; let those also who hate him flee before him."* **(Psalms. 68:1)**.

Therefore, O God, arise and let all your enemies in our lives be scattered in Jesus name!

It is written, *"and He that searches the hearts knows what the mind of the spirit is, because He makes intercession for the saints according to the will of God."* **(Romans 8:27)**

Therefore, the intercessory prayers of Jesus, who is seated on the right hand of the throne of God, will not be in vain over our lives, in the name of Jesus.

It is written, *"The Lord is your keeper; the Lord is the shade at your right hand. The sun shall not strike you by day, nor the moon by night. The Lord shall preserve you from all evil; He shall preserve your soul. The Lord shall preserve our going out and our coming in from this time forth, and even forevermore."* **(Psalms. 121:5-8)**

Therefore, O Lord, spread your covering of fire and the blood of Jesus over us and our loved ones, in the name of Jesus.

It is written, *"Rejoice always, pray without ceasing, in everything give thanks; for this is the will of God in Christ Jesus for you."* **(1 Thess. 5:16:18).**

Therefore, we thank you Father, for raising a spiritual shield over our loved ones and us. Thank you for giving us the heart for appreciating everything you are doing for us. Thank you for filling our hearts and our home with joy and peace that surpasses all understanding. Blessed be your name for all the answers to our prayers in the name of Jesus!

You are holy, holy, Lord God Almighty, who was and is and is to come, Amen!

O Lord, let our season of divine intervention appear in the name of Jesus!

O you gates in the heavenlies standing against our destiny, lift up your heads in the name of Jesus!

O you gates in the waters standing against our destiny, lift up your heads in the name of Jesus!

O you gates in the earth standing against our destiny, lift up your heads in the name of Jesus!

O you gates under the earth standing against our destiny, lift up your heads in the name of Jesus!

O God, arise and destroy every gate keeper assigned against our lives in the name of Jesus!

We break the backbone of every spirit of scarcity in our lives in the name of Jesus!

O Lord anoint our eyes to see divine opportunities in the name of Jesus!

Lord let every blindness to the treasures of our lives be cleared in the name of Jesus!

Let our divine helpers appear in the name of Jesus!

We declare, O Lord, that the rest of our lives will be better than the first part, in Jesus name!

We declare, O Lord that will overcome obstacles and defeat every enemy, in Jesus name!

We declare, O Lord that every blessing and promise that you put in our hearts will come to pass because this is our time for favor, in Jesus name!

We declare, O Lord that this is a new season of increase in our lives. We speak health, wisdom, creativity, divine connections, and supernatural opportunities. They are coming our way, in Jesus name!

We declare, O Lord that we choose faith over fear. We are victorious in faith, in Jesus name!

We declare, O Lord that that we are not just surviving, this is our time to thrive in prosperity, in Jesus name!

We declare, O Lord that we will believe that we have received in the spirit even though we do not see anything happening in the flesh, in Jesus name!

We declare, O Lord that our rewards are being transferred to us because we remain in faith, in Jesus name!

We declare, O Lord that doubt will not ruin our optimistic spirit, in Jesus name!

We declare, O Lord that we are prisoners of hope and get up every morning expecting your favor, in Jesus name!

We declare, O Lord that you will do amazing things in our lives, in Jesus name!

We declare, O Lord that we are closer to your abundant blessing than we think, our time has come, your promises will come to pass, in Jesus name!

We declare, O Lord that we will stay in an attitude of faith and expectation, in Jesus name!

We declare, O Lord that we are not worried, we know that you are our vindicator. It may seem to be taking a long time, but we will reap in due season if trust in you Lord, in Jesus name!

We declare, O Lord that you know the secret petitions our heart and we believe that they will come to fulfilment, in Jesus name!

We declare, O Lord that you will open new doors for us, in Jesus name!

We declare, O Lord that we will see your goodness, in Jesus name!

We declare, O Lord that this is our time to believe because favor is coming our way, in Jesus name!

We declare, O Lord that you have paved the way to abundant prosperity for us, prosperity more than we can every dream of or imagine, for your sake, in Jesus name!

We declare, O Lord that in your eyes our future is extremely bright, in Jesus name!

We declare, O Lord that we will rise higher and higher and see more of your favor and blessings and we will live the prosperous life you have in store for us, in Jesus name!

We declare, O Lord that we may have a lot of troubles, but we know that everything is going to be alright, in Jesus name!

We declare, O Lord that we have faith because we have put you first, in Jesus name!

We thank you, O Lord that our set time for favor is here, in Jesus name!

We declare, O Lord that our hour of deliverance has come, in Jesus name!

We declare, O Lord that there is no limit to what we can do, in Jesus name!

We declare, O Lord that there is no obstacle we cannot overcome, in Jesus name!

We declare, O Lord that that we have seen your accomplishments and they are good, in Jesus name!

We declare, O Lord that there is no challenge that is too great for us because you are with us, in Jesus name!

We declare, O Lord that you always succeed, in Jesus name!

We declare, O Lord that there is no financial difficulty or situation in our lives that is too great for you to resolve, in Jesus name!

We declare, O Lord that you are our Father Jehovah Jireh and that you own everything and you are our provider, in Jesus name!

We declare, O Lord that your promises declare that we are destined to live a victorious life, in Jesus name!

We declare, O Lord that we are your children, in Jesus name!

We declare, O Lord that the seeds of increase, success, and promotion are taking a new root; your favor will spring forth in our lives in a great way; we will see new seasons of blessings and new seasons of your favor. It's our time to have abundant faith, in Jesus name!

O Lord, it is written; according to your faith, it will be done unto you. Ps. 2:8 says *"ask me and I will give you the nations as your inheritance."*

Therefore, we ask you Lord to fulfil our highest hopes and dreams, in Jesus name!

We ask you this day, O Lord to give us our abundant blessing now, in Jesus name!

We dare to exercise our faith by asking you O Lord so that we may receive indeed, in Jesus name!

We thank you O Lord that for encouraging our faith, in Jesus name!

We declare, O Lord that this is our time for favor, in Jesus name!

We declare, O Lord that this is our time to prosper abundantly, in Jesus name!

We declare, O Lord that this is our time to have instant answers to prayer, in Jesus name!

We declare, O Lord that this is our time to ask and receive, in Jesus name!

We declare, O Lord that this is our time to thank you and testify for answered prayer, in Jesus name!

We declare, O Lord that we are blessed and that goodness and mercy are following us right now, in Jesus name!

We declare, O Lord that you favor is surrounding us like a shield – you prosper us even in the desert, in Jesus name!

We declare, O Lord that you have great things for us in the spirit and that you have already released favor into our prayers, in Jesus name!

We declare, O Lord that you are a great and Holy God, in Jesus name!

It is written, *"Delight yourself in the Lord and he will give you the desires of your heart."* **(Ps 37:4).**

We therefore declare, O Lord that we delight in you because you are our Father God and because we are your children you have made us the head and not the tail. You want to take us to a new level of prosperity, in Jesus name!

We declare, O Lord that because we are your children, we are more than conquerors, in Jesus name!

We declare, O Lord that we are blessed and you supply all our needs. We have more than enough, in Jesus name!

We declare, O Lord that we have abundant favor indeed, in Jesus name!

We declare, O Lord that we are filled indeed with the presence of the Holy Spirit, in Jesus name!

We declare, O Lord that we have abundant faith indeed, in Jesus name!

We declare, O Lord that you have answered our prayers, in Jesus name!

We declare, O Lord that our debts are all paid up, in Jesus name!

We declare, O Lord that we are healthy, in Jesus name!

We declare, O Lord that we have no lack and that we have more than enough, in Jesus name!

We declare, O Lord that we are extremely blessed so much that we can bless your kingdom, in Jesus name!

We declare, O Lord that we are extremely blessed so much that we can bless others, in Jesus name!

We declare, O Lord that we have entered into an anointing of ease, in Jesus name!

We declare, O Lord that for every opportunity we have missed, every chance we've blown, you will turn the clock and bring bigger and better things across our path, in Jesus name!

We declare, O Lord that we will not settle for less than your best, in Jesus name!

Please restore the time that we have lost, O Lord that, in Jesus name!

Restore our victories, O Lord, in Jesus name!

Restore our lost joy, lost peace, lost health, lost insight, lost faith, lost dedication, and desire to please you, we declare, O Lord in Jesus name!

We declare, O Lord that you use what was meant for our harm to our advantage, in Jesus name!

We declare, O Lord that you are a faithful God, in Jesus name!

We declare, O Lord that you will blossom our lives in ways that we can never imagine, in Jesus name!

We know, O Lord that you will bless us abundantly, in Jesus name!

We know, O Lord that you will provide divine connections, in Jesus name!

We declare, O Lord that we are not suffering – we are blessed, in Jesus name!

We declare, O Lord that our difficulties will give way to new growth, new opportunities, and new vision, in Jesus name!

O Lord let us see your blessing bloom in our lives in ways we would never dreamt possible, in Jesus name!

We declare, O Lord that we will stay in faith, so that what was meant to stop us will not be a stumbling block but a stepping stone taking us to a higher level, in Jesus name!

We declare, O Lord that we are not ordinary, but we are children of the most high God, in Jesus name!

We declare, O Lord that we created to rise above problems, in Jesus name!

We declare victory over strife O Lord, in Jesus name!

We declare, O Lord that no weapon formed against us shall prosper, in Jesus name!

We declare, O Lord that we are healthy and that no sickness shall live in us, in Jesus name!

We declare, O Lord that triumph is our birthright, in Jesus name!

We declare, O Lord that our setbacks are simply setups for greater comebacks that will place us to be better than we were before, in Jesus name!

We declare, O Lord that with you all things are possible, in Jesus name!

We declare, O Lord that we are in agreement with you. We know you have supernatural favor in store for us. You have supernatural opportunities, supernatural healing, and supernatural restoration, in Jesus name!

We declare, O Lord that you want to do unusual things in our lives, in Jesus name!

We declare, O Lord that in faith, we have expectation deep in our spirits, in Jesus name!

We declare, O Lord that this will not be a survival year but a supernatural year in which you will abundantly come through for us, in Jesus name!

We believe, O Lord that you have come through for us, in Jesus name!

We declare, O Lord that because we hope in you, we will not be put to shame, in Jesus name!

We declare, O Lord that your word is right and true, you are faithful in all you do, in Jesus name!

We declare, O Lord that you are our refuge and strength, an ever present helper, in Jesus name!

We declare, O Lord that we will cast our cares on you and you will sustain us, you will never let the righteous fall, in Jesus name!

We declare, O Lord that you are the strength of our hearts and our portion forever, in Jesus name!

We declare, O Lord that you are our dwelling, therefore, no harm will befall us, and no disaster will come near our tent, in Jesus name!

We declare, O Lord that you are our refuge and our fortress, in Jesus name!

We declare, O Lord that you will command your angels concerning us to guard us in all our ways, in Jesus name!

We declare, O Lord that even in darkness the light will dawn for us, in Jesus name!

We declare, O Lord that your word is eternal and stands firm in the heavens, in Jesus name!

We declare, O Lord that your faithfulness will continue throughout all generations, in Jesus name!

We declare, O Lord that you will keep us from harm; you will watch over our lives; you will watch over our coming and our going both now and for evermore, in Jesus name! **(Psalms. 121)**

Thank you O Lord for the assurance that you are watching over us even when we sleep, in Jesus name! **(Psalms. 13:5-6)**

We declare, O Lord that you will drive those that do evil away from us and that you will protect us from their influence, in Jesus name! **(Ps. 66:1-4)**

We will shout with joy to you O Lord, we will sing the glory of your name and make your praise glorious. How awesome are your deeds! So great is your power that your enemies cringe before you, in Jesus name!

We declare, O Lord that that we will give you thanks for you answered us, in Jesus name! **(Psalms. 118:21)**

We declare, O Lord that we will praise you with all our hearts; before the gods we will sing your praise. We will bow down towards your Holy temple and will praise your name for your love and your faithfulness, for you have exalted above all things, your name, and your word, in Jesus name! **(Psalms. 138:1-3)**

Why do We Pray?

We pray because it is our only means of communication with our Heavenly Father. As believers we are supposed to pray. It is written, *"And he spake a parable unto them to this end, that men ought always to pray, and not to faint."* **Luke18:1**

Prayer is one of the greatest commandment Jesus Christ left behind for us to practice daily. *"David said Evening, and morning, and at noon, will I pray, and cry aloud: and he shall hear my voice."* **Psalms55:17**.

Jesus Christ himself thought His disciples how to pray

"And it came to pass, that, as he was praying in a certain place, when he ceased, one of his disciples said unto him, Lord, teach us to pray, as John also taught his disciples.

And he said unto them, When ye pray, say, Our Father which art in heaven, Hallowed be thy name. Thy kingdom come. Thy will be done, as in heaven, so in earth.

Give us day by day our daily bread

"And forgive us our sins; for we also forgive every one that is indebted to us. And lead us not into temptation; but deliver us from evil." **Luke11:1-4**

I believe that daily prayers is necessary for daily survival. Every time we pray we open up our spirit man to receive any divine signal of warning, revelation, instructions and direction from the Lord.

We Don't Believe **(Hebrews 11:6, Romans 10:14)**

The Bible says, *"He that cometh to God must believe that He is, and that He is a rewarder of them that diligently seek Him."* **(Hebrews 11:6)**.

We must really believe "He is" or we will never come to Him in prayer. If we don't come to Him in prayer we inevitably don't really believe. We don't believe God will hear or answer our prayers. We either don't believe He is able to answer our prayer, our request is to big for Him, He can't handle it, He's too far removed (transcendent), or He doesn't really care enough to intervene on our behalf.

Paul wrote, *"How then shall they call on Him in whom they have not believed"* **(Romans 10:14)**.

We are unable or unmotivated to call on Him because of our unbelief. Think about it, if we knew if we asked Him for something right now He would grant it, would we not go to Him in prayer? Of course, any of us would.

The bible says those who know their God, they shall be strong and they shall do exploit.It is written Therefore, my beloved brethren, be ye stedfast, unmoveable, always abounding in the work of the Lord, forasmuch as ye know that your labour is not in vain in the Lord.

"God does care and desires to meet our every need" **(1 Peter 5:7, Philippians 4:19)**.

"We must correct our thinking and then we will be free to seek Him in prayer." **(Proverbs 23:7a)**.

Carnality and the Weakness of Our Flesh (Mark 14:37-38)

"The spirit is willing, but the flesh is weak" **(Mark 14:38)**. Our flesh is opposed to anything spiritual and will fight us all the way.

Paul said, *"For the flesh sets its desire against the Spirit, and the Spirit against the flesh, for these are in contrary to one another, so that you may not do the things that you please"* **(Galatians 5:17)**.

"If you want to see how weak your flesh is try praying for an entire hour" **(Mark 14:37)**.

We Lack the Spiritual Discipline

We may be saved, sanctified and Spirit-Filled, but without discipline we will never spend quality time with God in prayer.

The Psalmist wrote, *"Delight yourself in the Lord; And He will give you the desires of your heart. Commit your way to the Lord, Trust also in Him, and He will bring it to pass"* **(Psalms 37:4-5)**.

Notice the verses says, *"Delight yourself in the Lord, commit your way to the Lord."* Many have the desire to pray but never get around to it. We may delight in the Lord and desire to spend time with Him but it takes commitment and discipline if we are to follow through on our desire and spend time with Him in prayer. No one ever spends regular quality time in prayer without commitment and discipline.

We must have a resolve that nothing will get in our way of spending time with God. It will help to set apart a specific time for daily prayer. Once we get use to it, it will become easier and easier.

It is important that we don't give up if we happen to fall short and miss a day. If you miss one day just take up where you left off the next day and keep pressing on.

We've Left Our First Love

Jesus said to the church of Ephesus, *"I have this against you, that you have left your first love. Therefore remember from where you have fallen, and repent"* **(Revelation 2:4)**.

We no longer have that enjoyment of God's presence we once had. We have left our first love and must return. *"Oh, taste and see that the Lord is good; Blessed is the man who trusts in Him"* **(Psalms 34:8)**.

Like many couples, we start off loving spending time with each other and as time goes on we let the fire die out and spend less and less time with each other. At the beginning of the relationship nothing could keep us apart. It's the same with our relationship with God.

We have forgotten that *"In Your (His) presence is fullness of joy; at Your (His) right hand there are pleasures forever"* **(Psalms 16:11)**.

We Don't Want God Messing with Our Lives

Hudson Taylor said *"Whenever we truly get alone with God, He'll deal with our lives."* When we get alone with God in prayer, we put ourself in a place for God to work in our life.

"Like the rich young ruler He begins to put His finger on things in our life." **(Matthew 19:16-22)**.

Not to spend time in prayer shows we are unwilling for God to mess around in our life. Let's expose ourself to Him in prayer allowing Him to do what He desires in us. We will be the better for it.

There's Sin in Our Life

John Bunyon said, *"Prayer will make a man cease from sin as sin will entice a man to cease from prayer."*

Think about it, when we have had failure in any area, we are less likely to spend quality time with God. It's usually on our part. We feel guilty and unworthy and unmotivated to approach Him. This is why we must keep ourself in right standing and immediately make things right with Him when we have failed. **(1 John 1:5-9)**.

Actually, when we have failed, the first thing we should do is boldly run into His presence. The Bible says, *"Let us therefore come boldly unto the throne of grace, that we may obtain mercy, and find grace to help in time of need"* **(Hebrews 4:16)**.

Notice, we are to approach the throne of grace with boldness in order to obtain mercy and find grace. To obtain mercy denotes we have messed up in someway and therefore we are in need of mercy. When we have failed, let's boldly run to Him instead of running away from Him.

Laziness

Prayer is often laborious. It was said of Epaphras that he was *"always labouring fervently for you in prayers"* **(Colossians 4:12)**. Prayer takes effort and work if we are praying as we ought.

Paul requested of the Romans, *"I beseech you, brethren, for the Lord Jesus Christ's sake, and for the love of the Spirit, that you strive together with me in your prayers to God for me"* **(Romans 15:30)**.

We must strive in prayer to God. Therefore, our lack of prayer is often the result of laziness.

We are exhorted, *"not slothful (lazy or sluggish) in business, fervent in spirit, serving the Lord"* **(Romans 12:11)**.

"That ye be not slothful (lazy or sluggish), but followers of them who through faith and patience inherit the promises" **(Hebrews 6:12)**.

Prayer demands thought, concentration, effort, resolve and persistence. Let's discipline ourselves in seeking the face of God.

Isaiah cried, *"There is none that calleth upon Thy name, that stirreth up himself to take hold of Thee"* **(Isaiah 64:7)**. Let's stir ourselves to lay hold of God with all we have within us.

Other engagement take priority Over Prayer

We don't have time to pray or more accurately, we don't make time to pray. Other things take priority over prayer. This is proof of idolatry **(1 John 5:21)**. We are to *"seek first His kingdom and His righteousness"* **(Matthew 6:33)**.

Even those in full time ministry let things sneak in to rob us from spending quality time with God in prayer – sermon preparation, visitation, church administration, counseling, etc.

These things are often spiritual in nature. Nothing should take priority over time with the Lord. Martin Luther said, *"I have so much to do that I shall have to spend the first three hours in prayer."*

We are Faint Hearted

Jesus said, *"Men ought always to pray, and not to faint"* **(Luke 18:1)**. We can often become fainthearted when we don't see the results to our prayers right away. We get discouraged and give up.

Jesus goes on to teach us a parable of a widow who goes to an unjust judge seeking help. The judge seems to ignore and refuse to listen to her.

She is undaunted by his refusal and relentlessly continues going to him with her request until he says, *"Though I do not fear God nor regard man, yet because this widow troubles me I will avenge her, lest by her continual coming she weary me"* **(Luke 18:4-5)**.

Jesus went on to say, *"Hear what the unjust judge said. And shall God not avenge His own elect who cry out day and night to Him, though He bears long with them? I tell you that He will avenge them speedily. Nevertheless, when the Son of Man comes, will He really find faith on the earth"* **(Luke 18:6-8)**

Jesus is challenging us in this parable not to ever give up. Though the answer to our prayer does not come immediately, we are to continue seeking God until we see the results we are seeking. This persistence in prayer is the type of faith God is looking for in His people.

We Lack the Spirit of Prayer

The Holy Spirit is the Spirit of Prayer. Paul wrote, *"You have not received the spirit of bondage again to fear, but you have received the Spirit of adoption whereby we cry out, Abba, Father"* **(Romans 8:15)**.

"Because you are sons, God has sent forth the Spirit of His Son into your hearts, crying, "Abba, Father" **(Galatians 4:6)**.

When we are adopted into the family of God through the new birth, God's Spirit begins to reside within us and cries out to the Father in prayer. If we do not have a sense of the Holy Spirit crying out to God from within us we may not have received His Spirit through the new birth.

If we have been born again and we aren't stirred by the Spirit of prayer, perhaps we need a fresh charge of this Spirit of Prayer or we need to be filled anew with the Holy Ghost. Let's ask God to fill us afresh and anew with His Holy Spirit. When we are filled with the Holy Ghost, we will find the Spirit of God crying out from within us in prayer and praise.

"Disciplining ourselves with time in God's Word and prayer will help to rekindle this in our life" **(Ephesians 5:18-19 and Colossians 3:16)**. I have noticed, the more time I spend in prayer, the more I sense the Holy Spirit crying out from within me to God.

Prayer: *Father, forgive me for my lack of faith, for letting things take priority over spending time with You, for being negligent in my prayer life, and becoming faint hearted. Please fill me with Your Holy Spirit and help me to seek You in prayer as I should. In Jesus' name, Amen!*

Stages of Salvation

Justification is when the soul is set free from the penalty of sin. 1 John 1:9 – "If we confess our sins, he is faithful and just and will forgive us our sins and purify us from all unrighteousness."

Sanctification is when the soul is set free from the power of sin. **John 17:17** – *"For this is the will of God, even your sanctification."*

Glorification is when the soul is set free from the possibility of sin.

1 John 1:3 – *"Dear friends, now we are children of God, and what we will be has not yet been made known. But we know that when he appears, we shall be like him."*

We enter the door of sanctification the moment we consecrate our lives to Christ and submit ourselves to the process of becoming more like Him. Justification and sanctification are pre-requisites for glorification when salvation is finally complete. Glorification occurs after the death of the body when the soul is transported beyond the reach of temptation and sin. Salvation is not complete until we have been glorified.

Philippians 1:6 says, *"He who has started a good work in you will carry it on to completion."* But, God seems to have tempered his own sovereignty by gifting man with free will.

Christians are certainly eternally secure, but this security is conditional. It could be disrupted by the sovereignty of God or the free will God has given man. Can a man lose his salvation? I don't think so. **Romans 8:38** says, *"For I am convinced that nothing can ever separate us from God's love."*

Paul goes on to list all of the things that are incapable of separating us from God's love.

But, Paul does not include ourselves in that list. Can a man choose to become an apostate? The Bible seems to indicate that a man can choose to walk away from God.

There are at least 80 passages in the New Testament that teach that the process of salvation can be interrupted, delayed or stopped altogether. **Jude 21** says, *"keep yourselves in God's love"* and **Jude 24** says, *"He is able to keep you."*

This seems to indicate a conditional relationship. He will keep us if we will determine to be kept.

Jesus declared himself to be the true vine. Dead branches are cut away and destroyed while fruitful branches are pruned so they will produce even more fruit **(John 15:4)**. Christ warns against the prevalent teaching of cheap grace.

Hebrews 10:26-27 says, *"If we deliberately keep on sinning after we have received the knowledge of the truth, no sacrifice for sins is left, but only a fearful expectation of judgment and of raging fire that will consume the enemies of God."*

1 Peter 2:20 says, *"It would have been better for them not to have known the way of righteousness, than to have known it and then to turn their backs on the sacred command that was passed on to them."*

Peter is saying that people who enter the way and then departed from it are worse off. This is contradictory for those who argue that we might continue to live a sinful lifestyle and still be rewarded with eternal life. If they received eternal life how are they worse off?

I question the idea that we cannot walk away from God because it seems to make God inconsistent. Either he has gifted us with free will or he has not. But I argue that it is very unlikely that a man would choose to walk away from God if he were truly, genuinely saved.

Maybe a more accurate statement would be not so much, *"once saved always saved"* but *"if saved always saved."*

CHAPTER 1
Prevailing Prayer

"Elias was a man subject to like passions as we are, and he prayed earnestly that it might not rain: and it rained not on the earth by the space of three years and six months. And he prayed again, and the heaven gave rain, and the earth brought forth her fruit." **James 5:17-18**

Often some folks argue about the effectiveness and efficiency of prevailing prayer. I have had some great times in prayers before God Almighty. I have occasion where I prayed and I could sense it within myself, yes, I have prayed to a very deep level. Such prayer was not premediated or planed that way. Every time we travail in prayers, it prevail with answers.

Prevailing prayers are directional and instructional. What do I mean? Even as you are praying God is revealing deep secret to you. The more we engage in prevailing prayers the more God gives us direction,, instruction , correction in righteousness in the midst of our prayers.

Chapter 1 - Prevailing Prayer

Elijah heard from God and prayed accordingly. *"The word of the Lord came to Elijah"* **(1 Kings 18:1)**. And again, *"Let it be known, I have done all these things at thy word"* **(1 Kings 18:36)**.

Prevailing prayer should be directional. As long as God is the one leading us, we cannot miss it. *"God how do you want me to pray?"*

I'm convinced that if we would wait on direction from God first, seeking Him and as we receive word from Him, pray accordingly, we would have much more effective prayers.

Prevailing prayer must depend on the Holy Spirit, be made in accordance with **(Romans 8:26-27, 1 John 5:14-15)** and the goal of seeing God's will implemented in the affairs of men on earth **Matthew 6:10**.

We must pray in the name of the Lord **(James 5:14)**.

There is power in Jesus' name. So much that God, *"Bestowed on Him a name that is above every name, that at the name of Jesus every knee should bow, and every tongue confess that Jesus Christ is Lord, to the glory of God the father"* **(Philippians 2:10-11)**.

Praying in His name is not simply a blank check that we sign to get whatever we want. Praying in the name of the Lord Jesus means four things:

We receive power of attorney

If you are given power of attorney over someone's estate, you are to use the assets for their purposes only. That said, you can use it however you choose. However, there will be a day when you will have to give an account as to how you used the funds. Likewise, there will be an accounting of how we used His name.

Chapter 1 - Prevailing Prayer

We pray in God's will *(1 John 5:14-15)*

Praying in His name means we are praying for His purposes (will) to be implemented in the affairs of men (our affairs and life) on earth **(Matthew 6:10)**.

We pray in His merit as opposed to our own *(Romans 5:1-2, Hebrews 4:16)*

When we come to Him, praying in His name, we come in His merit and not our own. We come in His righteousness, having been made worthy by His finished work on the cross for us **(2 Corinthians 5:21)**.

We pray for God's glory **(John 14:13)**. When praying in His name we should be praying for that which will bring Him glory. Judge what you are praying for and if it will bring God glory then you are praying rightly and if not don't pray for it.

Praying must be done in faith *(James 5:15, James 1:6-8)*

Jesus said if we have faith we can move mountains **(Mark 11:22-24)**. Below are a few things that will help strengthen your faith.

Be divinely directed *(1 John 5:14-15)*

Elijah was filled with faith because he knew he was in God's will and acting according to His word.

Read the Word (Romans 10:17). Spending time reading the Bible builds and strengthens our faith.

Meditate *(Psalm 1:2-3 and Joshua 1:8)*

Like I say all the time, we need more than mere reading of scripture. We must spend time not only reading the Word, but also in meditation. This means we take a passage, verse or phrase and toss it over and over in our mind, letting it sink deep within our spirit. This will build and strengthen our faith.

Use your imagination *(John 5:17 and 19)*

Visualize God doing what you're praying for and see it as completed. Jesus saw what the Father was doing in the spiritual realm before He did anything, and then acted accordingly. If we really believe something, our imagination will be stirred which will also stir our faith.

Chapter 1 - Prevailing Prayer

Pray in the Spirit

Jude said, *"But you, beloved, building yourselves up on your most holy faith, praying in the Holy Spirit" (Jude 20). Paul said, "Praying always with all prayer and supplication in the Spirit, and watching thereunto with all perseverance and supplication for all saints"* **(Ephesians 6:18)**.

Be bold when praying **(1 Kings 17:1, 18:44)**.

Elijah was bold in two ways:

He was confident in his declaration, and in what he believed God was going to do. Then he declared it.

He was bold in what he prayed for:

Elijah prayed that it wouldn't rain until he said it would **(1 Kings 17:1)**.

He prayed expecting liftto come back into the widow's son **(1 Kings 17:19-22)**.

There had been a drought for three and a half years. Elijah dared believe God would make it rain again.

If we are afraid to exercise boldness in our prayer life, we will never experience great effects from our prayers. **Psalms 81:10** says, *"Open thy mouth wide and I will fill it."*

George Mueller said this meant we should *"open our mouth wide in big requests."*

Pray specifically

There is a difference between communing and fellowshipping with God and asking God for things to be accomplished for His glory. Elijah needed to see something happen.

He didn't pray in general, *"Lord do something to turn the people around."* He sought the mind of God, asked how He wanted to pray, then prayed exactly the way He said. If we are to pray effectively, we must be specific in what we are praying for.

Chapter 1 - Prevailing Prayer

***Pray fervently** (James 5:16-18)*

Fervent means to *"work hard at, hot, boiling over, to put all you have into your praying."* If you are ever in a really desperate place and need someone's help, you won't calmly say to them, *"Would you mind helping me for a minute?"* No, you'd raise your voice (scream) and say, *"Help me now!"*

The early church prayed fervently for Peter and God sent an angel and miraculously delivered him out of jail and from the hand of Herod **(Acts 12:1-17)**.

It was said of Jesus, *"Who in the days of His flesh, when he had offered up prayers and supplication with strong crying and tears unto Him that was able to save Him from death, and was heard in that He feared"* **(Hebrews 5:7)**.

God told Isaiah, *"Put me in remembrance; let us argue our case together; state your cause that you may be proved right"* **(Isaiah 43:26).** Let's remind God of His Word and put all we have into our praying.

Be persistent *(1 Kings 17:19-21, 18:41-44)*

Whatever you're praying for you must not loose heart and give up. True faith believes when we have prayed, we have already received what we have asked for **(Mark 11:22-24)** and goes on to continue to ask and remind God of our request until the answer to our request has materialized.

Scriptural examples of persistence in prayer:

The widow's son **(1 Kings 17:19-21)**.

Elijah praying for rain **(1 Kings 18:41-44)**.

The Syrophonician woman **(Mark 7:24-30)**.

Jacob **(Genesis 32)**.

A friend asking for bread at midnight **(Luke 11:5-10)**.

The widow and the unjust judge **(Luke 18:1-8)**.

Pray with anticipation **(1 Kings 18:41-45)**.

Chapter 1 - Prevailing Prayer

When Elijah began to pray for it to rain again, after being dry for three and a half years, he prayed with expectancy. He put his head between his legs and prayed. He then asked his servant if he saw anything. He said, "there is nothing". He did this seven times, until after the seventh time the servant said, I see a cloud about the size of a man's hand.

When Elijah heard this, he knew the rain was on its way. Pray and keep praying in faith, looking for and expecting your answer, until it manifest itself.

***The one praying must be righteous** (James 5:16)*

The blind man who had been healed said, *"We know that God does not hear sinners"* **(John 9:31)**. Sins blocks our prayers from being heard and answered **(Isaiah 59:1-2; Psalms 66:18)**.

It's extremely important to understand we have absolutely no righteousness of our own **(Isaiah 64:6; Romans 3:23)**.

The only righteousness we will ever have is imputed righteousness **(2 Corinthians 5:21)**. That is why we need Jesus. He is the substitution for our sins. The moment we put our faith in Jesus as our only hope of salvation and the one who paid the penalty for our sins, we are declared righteous by God.

Jesus' righteousness is put to our account and we are righteous in God's sight. He sees us just as if we had never sinned. From that point on you can pray effectively as a righteous man or woman.

We also should daily ask God to search our heart for anything that may not be right with Him and make it right by confessing it as sin **(1 John 1:9)**. This should be done at the beginning of our prayer time.

We should also ask God to show us anything that might be wrong between us and any other person. If there is anything, we should do our best to make things right with them as well. This assures there is nothing standing in the way of our praying effectively.

Chapter 1 - Prevailing Prayer

"Therefore if you bring your gift to the altar, and there remember that your brother has something against you, 24 leave your gift there before the altar, and go your way. First be reconciled to your brother, and then come and offer your gift" **(Matthew 5:23-24)**.

If anyone has done us wrong or offended us in anyway, we must forgive them.

"Whenever you stand praying, if you have anything against anyone, forgive him" **(Mark 11:25)**.

"Moreover if your brother sins against you, go and tell him his fault between you and him alone. If he hears you, you have gained your brother" **(Matthew 18:15)**.

CHAPTER 2
WHAT ARE HINDRANCES TO PRAYER

"for from the first day that thou didst set thine heart to understand, and to chasten thyself before thy God, thy words were heard, and I am come for thy words"
Daniel 10:12

To have an effective prayer life we must remove all hindrances to our prayers. If our bank account is overdrawn, the first thing we do is try to find the accounting error and fix it. If our car won't start we take it to a mechanic to trouble-shoot the problem and then repair the car. If a businessman discovers he's running a loss he does a thorough investigation to find the culprit and correct it. Even so, if our prayer life isn't being fruitful we must find the root cause and reverse it.

As we look at possible hindrances to prayer, we inevitably must deal with negatives. However, the reverse side to every negative is a positive.

As we explore hindrances to prayer, let's deal with the negative, but not forget to focus on the alternate positive.

Here are a few hindrances to an effective and fruitful prayer life:

Having a Wrong Relationship with God

The Bible says, *"For if, when we were enemies, we were reconciled to God by the death of His Son, much more, being reconciled, we shall be saved by His life"* **(Romans 5:10)**. Prior to coming to Christ we were at enmity with God.

The first and primary hindrance we must clear up is our relationship with God. We do this by being *"reconciled to Him (God) through the death of His Son."* The moment we come to Jesus for forgiveness and reconciliation, we are no longer enemies but beloved children.

The opposite of having a wrong relationship with God is maintaining a close and intimate relationship with Him.

Chapter 2 - What are Hinrances to Prayer

This is the first step in having a good and fruitful prayer life. Much of our prayer time should be consumed in communing with God. As we spend regular time in fellowship with the Lord, developing a right relationship with Him, we will begin to discover our prayer life being more and more effective.

Having Sin in Our Lives

Sin is a barrier to fellowship with God and a major hindrance in our prayer life. The Psalmist said, *"If I regard iniquity in my heart, The Lord will not hear me"* **(Psalms 66:18)**. To regard is to esteem, care for and hold dear to our heart. It is not necessarily something we did or fell into once but something we cling to.

It is something we are clinging to and won't let go of. It may or may not be something that is outwardly visible to others, but something of the heart.

Isaiah said, *"Behold, the LORD's hand is not shortened, That it cannot save; Nor His ear heavy, That it cannot hear. But your iniquities have separated you from your God; And your sins have hidden His face from you, So that He will not hear"* **(Isaiah 59:1-2)**.

Sin must be dealt with and taken to the cross. If we confess our sins, He is faithful and just to forgive us our sins and to cleanse us from all unrighteousness **(1 John 1:9)**.

Looking on the positive side, *"If we walk in the light (of His exposure) as He is in the light, we have fellowship with one another, and the blood of Jesus Christ His Son cleanses us from all sin"* **(1 John 1:7)**.

Don't hide or cling to sin of any kind but immediately bring it before God, confessing it, and let the blood of Jesus cleanse you of all sin. We should continually be asking God to turn His search light on in our heart to expose any area where we may be falling short. This is consistent with maintaining a right relationship with God.

Chapter 2 - What are Hinrances to Prayer

Not Believing God

Do we really believe and expect God to intervene and answer our prayers. Faith is the primary key to answered prayer. Paul said, *"How then shall they call on Him in whom they have not believed."* **(Romans 10:14)**

James wrote concerning prayer, We must, *"Ask in faith without any doubting, for the one who doubts is like the surf of the sea, driven and tossed by the wind. For that man ought not to expect that he will receive anything from the Lord, being a double-minded man, unstable in all his ways"* **(James 1:5-8)**. Clearly unbelief is a major hindrance to prayer.

On the other hand, faith is a great asset to an effective prayer life. If unbelief is a hindrance then faith promotes powerful praying. Jesus said faith has the power to move mountains **(Mark 11:22-24)**. He said, *"All things you ask in prayer, believing, you will receive"* **(Matthew 21:22)**.

There is power in believing God. Let's spend time cultivating and building our faith so we can believe God for great things. Below are a few ways to build strong faith.

"Pray in accord with His will" **(1 John 5:14-15)**. When we know we are praying in line with His will, we can have faith and confidence He will grant the petitions we desire of Him.

Study the Word **(Romans 10:17)**. Spending time in the Word of God helps build and strengthen our faith. Read and study it.

Meditate on the Word **(Psalm 1:2-3 and Joshua 1:8)**. We need more than a casual reading of the scripture. We must spend time not only reading the Word but meditating on it. This means we take a passage, verse or phrase and toss it over and over in our mind, letting it sink deep within our spirit. This will build and strengthen our faith.

"Use your imagination" **(John 5:17 and 19)**. See God doing what you're praying for.

Chapter 2 - What are Hinrances to Prayer

See it as a done deal. Jesus saw what the Father was doing in the spiritual realm before He did anything and then acted accordingly. If we really believe something our imagination will be stirred and our imagination will stir our faith.

Pray in the Spirit. Jude said, *"But you, beloved, building yourselves up on your most holy faith, praying in the Holy Spirit"* **(Jude 20)**.

Having Idols in Your Life

God demands to be first in our life **(Matthew 6:33 and Exodus 20:3)**. We must not allow anything to take priority in our life above Him. If we do it is idolatry.

The elders of Israel came to Ezekiel to inquire of God and God spoke to Ezekiel saying, *"Son of man, these men have set up idols in their hearts and put wicked stumbling blocks before their faces. Should I let them inquire of me at all"* **(Ezekiel 14:3)**

God would not even listen to their prayers because they had "set up idols in their hearts." In contrast, if we are putting God first in our life, our prayers will flow before the throne of grace unhindered.

Neglecting to Pray

James said, *"You have not, because you ask not"* **(James 4:2)**. Neglect is inevitably a great hindrance to prayer. Someone will say, *"But God knows what I want without my asking. He will do what He wants anyway."* Of course He does, but God wants us to ask. Though God desires certain things for His children, He refuses to act until we ask.

Isaiah cried, *"There is none that calls upon Thy name, that stirs up himself to take hold of Thee"* **(Isaiah 64:7)**.

The writer of Hebrews wrote, *"Let us therefore come boldly unto the throne of grace, that we may obtain mercy, and find grace to help in time of need"* **(Hebrews 4:16)**.

Chapter 2 - What are Hinrances to Prayer

"Let's spend time laying hold of God and telling Him what we need and desire." **(Psalms 37:4-5)**

Wrong Motives

James wrote, *"You ask, and receive not, because you ask amiss, that you may consume it upon your lusts"* **(James 4:3)**. We so often pray with wrong motives. We go to God in prayer thinking, *"I don't care what God desires as long as I get what I want."*

Prayer is about implementing God's will in the affairs of men **(Matthew 6:10 and 1 John 5:14-15)**. It's for His purposes and His glory **(John 14:13-14)**. Let's make sure our motives are right when we seek Him in prayer. If we do, we will find our prayers unfettered.

Indifference to God's Word

When beginning our first church, I went to visit a young man who had missed a few services. He began to complain that God wasn't answering his prayers.

I asked if he had been spending time in God's Word. He said he hadn't. I quoted **Proverbs 28:9**, *"He who turns away his ear from listening to the law (Word), Even his prayer is an abomination."* Then I looked him in the eye and said, *"Case settled!"*

Spending time in the Word is the key to a powerful prayer life. Jesus said, *"If you maintain a living communion with Me and My words are at home in you, I command you to ask, at once, something for yourself, whatever your heart desires, and it will become yours"* **(John 15:7 – Wuest Expanded Translation)**.

The Word is paramount to maintaining a living communion with the God, praying in accord with His will and maintaining an effective prayer life. *See also James 1:22-25; Hebrews 2:1-3; 1 Peter 2:2; Psalms 1:2-3; Joshua 1:8.*

Chapter 2 - What are Hinrances to Prayer

Having an Unforgiving Spirit

Jesus said, *"Whenever you stand praying, forgive, if you have anything against anyone"* **(Mark 11:25)**.

If you harbor resentment and unforgiveness toward anyone or anything, including situations and even God, it will greatly hinder your prayer life. You may have been legitimately wronged, but we must forgive as God has forgiven us.

Paul wrote, *"Let all bitterness, and wrath, and anger, and clamour, and evil speaking, be put away from you, with all malice: And be ye kind one to another, tenderhearted, forgiving one another, even as God for Christ's sake hath forgiven you"* **(Ephesians 4:31-32)**.

A forgiving spirit is essential to a good prayer life. *See also Matthew 18:21-35; Colossians 3:13.*

Wrongs Unrighted

Jesus said, *"Therefore if you bring your gift to the altar, and there remember that your brother has something against you, leave your gift there before the altar, and go your way. First be reconciled to your brother, and then come and offer your gift"* **(Matthew 5:23-24)**.

Jesus was essentially saying, before you go to God in prayer, do your best to make things right with anyone who thinks you have wronged them in anyway. It doesn't mean they are necessarily right, but just if they think you have wronged them. If so, do your best to make amends with them. It's up to them if they will accept your apology or not. You must simply make a sincere attempt before God and the rest is up to them.

The opposite stands true. If someone has offended you, you must go to them and attempt to make things right.

Chapter 2 - What are Hinrances to Prayer

Jesus said, *"If your brother sins against you, go and tell him his fault between you and him alone. If he hears you, you have gained your brother"* **(Matthew 18:15)**.

Notice he said, *"If he hears you."* He may or may not listen to you. It is your responsibility to go to him nonetheless, with hopes they will reconcile with you. You must take care to go to them in the right way. You must not go to them in pride and arrogance, but in humility. As we try to be in right relationships with all we know, we will see our prayer life flourish.

Not Keeping Your Marriage Strong
(1 Peter 3:1-7)

In addressing the relationship between a husband and wife, Peter ends by saying, *"That your prayers will not be hindered"* **(1 Peter 3:7)**. The relationship of a married couple can be very powerful in the spiritual realm. It can also be a great hindrance if the relationship is not right.

This is why the devil does all he can to come between a couple and make them at odds with one another.

This is also why it is imperative we do all we can to deepen our relationship with each other, fight for one another and quickly reconcile when ever there is strife or disagreement. This is true physically, emotionally, spiritually and even sexually. **(1 Corinthians 7:1-5)**.

Let's fight for our marriage relationships *"That your prayers will not be hindered"* **(1 Peter 3:7)** but flourish.

Stinginess in Our Giving

The wise man wrote, *"He who shuts his ear to the cry of the poor will also cry himself and not be answered"* **(Proverbs 21:13)**. There is something about generosity that touches the heart of God. No, we can't buy the favor of God, but liberality in our giving and attitude reveals something about our heart.

When we give liberally, with a right attitude, it releases the power and generosity of God in every aspect of life. We reap what we have sown. Diligently study Malachi 3:8-12; Luke 6:36-38; 2 Corinthians 9:6-10; 2 Corinthians 9:11-15; Galatians 6:6-10; 1 John 3:16-22.

Satanic Resistance

We are in a constant struggle with the powers of darkness **(Ephesians 6:10-12)**. They will fight us every step of the way.

Daniel had been fasting and praying for twenty-one days when an angel appeared to him saying, *"Do not be afraid, Daniel, for from the first day that you set your heart on understanding this and on humbling yourself before your God, your words were heard, and I have come in response to your words. But the prince of the kingdom of Persia was withstanding me for twenty-one days; then behold, Michael, one of the chief princes, came to help me, for I had been left there with the kings of Persia"* **(Daniel 10:12-13)**.

There was a spiritual battle raging from the time he first began praying. The devil hates praying people.

This is why we must engage in spiritual warfare. Prayer is more than just asking and receiving, it is a spiritual battle. We must bind the strong man and all that stands against us **(Mark 3:27, Matthew 16:19, 18:18-20)**; join in agreement with other believers **(Matthew 18:18-20, Acts 4:23-24, 12:5; 12:12)**; pray in the spirit **(1 Corinthians 14:2)**; persist in prayer **(Genesis 32; Luke 18:1-8; Daniel 10:12-13)**; and yes, even fast as Daniel did if we are to gain ground in prayer.

Let's not sit back casually letting the devil attack us but aggressively fight in prayer until we have been triumphant over every foe.

"From the days of John the Baptist until now the kingdom of heaven suffers violence, and violent men take it by force." **(Matthew 11:12)**.

Chapter 2 - What are Hinrances to Prayer

Prayer: Lord Jesus, we humbly come before You asking You to remove all hindrances to us having a productive prayer life. Please forgive us for the hindrances we have allowed to come into our life. We commit to prayer afresh and anew. Increase our faith so we can once again believe You for great things. In Jesus name we pray, Amen!

Every Christian should desire to be more like Jesus. One of the most effective ways to be more like Him is to emulate His prayer life.

"He that says he abides in Him ought himself also so to walk, even as He walked" **(1 John 2:6)**.

"Therefore be imitators of God, as beloved children" **(Ephesians 5:1)**.

JESUS STYLE OF PRAYER

He prayed early in the morning. *"And in the morning, rising up a great while before day, He went out and departed into a solitary place, and there prayed"* **(Mark 1:35)**.

Jesus put the Father first, rising early in the morning to spend time with Him and so must we. We must give Him the first of our day before we do anything else.

Jesus rose early in the morning to seek the face of God. If we are to emulate Jesus we also must begin our day with prayer. Joshua began his day seeking God and as a result won the battle against Jericho **(Joshua 3:1 and 5:13-15)**.

We must seek the face of God first thing before the day's battle begins. Jesus knew this and that's why He rose early to pray before the day's battle began. We too must rise early to pray following Jesus' example.

He prayed in a solitary. Jesus *"departed into a solitary place, and there prayed"* **(Mark 1:35)**.

There are times to pray publicly, but we need regular times alone with God as well.

Chapter 2 - What are Hinrances to Prayer

Jesus said, *"But thou, when thou prayest, enter into thy closet, and when thou hast shut thy door, pray to thy Father which is in secret; and thy Father which seeth in secret shall reward thee openly"* **(Matthew 6:6).**

Jesus knew to have quality time with the Father He had to be completely alone where there would be no interruptions or distractions. It's in the solitary place that our relationship with God is developed. I find in the early hours of the morning my time with God is less likely to be interrupted.

If we are to pray like Jesus prayed, we must have a daily time of solitude where we are not distracted by phones, computers or anything else.

He prayed fervently. *"Who in the days of his flesh, when he had offered up prayers and supplications with strong crying and tears unto him that was able to save him from death, and was heard in that he feared"* **(Hebrews 5:7).**

He put His entire self (emotionally, spiritually, mentally and His flesh) into His praying. He prayed until He was exhausted and had to have an angel come to strengthen Him **(Luke 22:43)**. It's usually in times of great distress that we pray the most fervently. Jesus was no different.

When facing the greatest battle of His life it was said of Him, *"And being in agony He was prayed the more fervently"* **(Luke 22:44)**.

The early church emulated this facing threats for preaching the gospel, *"They lifted their voices to God with one accord"* **(Acts 4:24)**.

When facing trouble with Peter's arrest, *"Peter was kept in the prison, but prayer for him was being made fervently by the church to God"* **(Acts 12:5)**. If we are going to imitate Jesus' prayer life we must put everything we have into our praying.

Chapter 2 - What are Hinrances to Prayer

Jesus prayed with dependency upon the Holy Spirit. *"The Spirit also helps our weakness; for we do not know how to pray as we should, but the Spirit Himself intercedes for us with groanings too deep for words"* **(Romans 8:26)**.

Jesus always prayed with dependency upon God's Spirit and we are instructed to do the same. We cannot pray adequately on our own.

Jesus said, *"Apart from Me you can do nothing"* **(John 15:5)**. We too must pray with complete dependency upon the Spirit of God. See How to Pray in the Spirit.

He prayed in accordance with God's will. Jesus, being God in the flesh, knew the mind and will of God perfectly and always prayed accordingly. If we are to pray like Jesus we must pray according to God's will. In so doing we are assured of having our request heard.

John wrote, *"And this is the confidence that we have in Him, that, if we ask any thing according to His will, He heareth us: And if we know that He hear us, whatsoever we ask, we know that we have the petitions that we desired of Him"* **(1 John 5:14-15)**.

The only way we can be sure we are praying in God's will is to pray the Word of God – His revealed will. We must diligently study the Word of God to know how to pray in accord with His will **(2 Timothy 2:15)**.

It's a good practice to find scripture that pertains to your situation and begin praying the Word of God over it. We can never go wrong using the Word — in so doing, we can be assured we are praying as Jesus prayed.

He prayed in faith. Jesus said, *"All things, whatsoever ye shall ask in prayer, believing, ye shall receive"* **(Matthew 21:22)**.

Chapter 2 - What are Hinrances to Prayer

Again He said, *"Have faith in God. For verily I say unto you, That whosoever shall say unto this mountain, Be thou removed, and be thou cast into the sea; and shall not doubt in his heart, but shall believe that those things which he saith shall come to pass; he shall have whatsoever he saith. Therefore I say unto you, What things soever ye desire, when ye pray, believe that ye receive them, and ye shall have them"* **(Mark 11:22-24)**.

Jesus always prayed in faith, knowing God heard and would grant His request. When we pray according to God's will (as revealed through His Word) we can pray with faith knowing God desires to answer our prayers.

We are to put God in remembrance of His Word **(Isaiah 43:26)** and we can come into agreement with the Word of God in prayer **(Matthew 18:19)**, knowing He magnifies His Word above His name **(Psalm 138:2)**.

He visualized God answering His prayer. Jesus said, *"Truly, truly, I say to you, the Son can do nothing of Himself, unless it is something He sees the Father doing"* **(John 5:19)**.

Before Jesus acted or prayed He visualized the Father doing it in the spiritual realm. As a result, it materialized in the natural realm. Likewise, we must see God doing the very thing we are asking of Him, which also stimulates our faith.

Jesus prayed with persistence. It was said of Jesus that He *"prayed the third time, saying the same words"* **(Matthew 26:44)**.

Jesus prayed the same thing multiple times. He was persistent in His praying. We are not to use vain repetition, however, there is a difference between repetition and vain repetition. We can vocalize meaningless words in our prayers and people often do (like the Pharisees). There is also meaningful repetition like Jesus prayed.

Chapter 2 - What are Hinrances to Prayer

He prayed persistently the same thing until He had the breakthrough He needed and desired. We see persistent praying taught and exemplified throughout scripture.

Elijah stretched himself out over the widow's son three times until his life returned to him **(1 Kings 17:19-21)**; Elijah prayed for rain and had his servant look for a sign of rain seven times **(1 Kings 18:41-44)**; The Syrophonician woman kept crying out to Jesus **(Mark 7:24-30)**; Jacob wrestled with God until He blessed him **(Genesis 32)**; A friend asking for bread at midnight **(Luke 11:5-10)**; And the widow and the unjust judge **(Luke18:1-8)**.

Let's lay hold of God in persistent prayer and not let anything deter us until we've received what we are requesting of God **(Isaiah 64:7)**. In so doing, we will be emulating Jesus' prayer life.

CONCLUSION

"Moreover, as for me, God forbid that I should sin against the Lord in ceasing to pray for you: but I will teach you the good and the right way." **1 Samuel 12:23**

Unless otherwise stated, we must all come unto repentance if we must encounter our savior Jesus Christ. Repentance is the key to deliverance, protection, and promotion. If you love to see testimonies in your life, I encourage you to repent of your sins. Confess the Lord Jesus as your savior.

"Let us hear the conclusion of the whole matter: Fear God, and keep his commandments: for this is the whole duty of man.
For God shall bring every work into judgment, with every secret thing, whether it be good, or whether it be evil."

Eccl 12:13-14

The entire book will remain a story to everyone who is not ready to make a decision for Jesus Christ.

Chapter 2 - What are Hinrances to Prayer

One man said if you failed to plan we have planned to fail in life. We want you to make plans to make heaven. The bible says in **eccl:12:14**, *"For God shall bring every work into judgment, with every secret thing, whether it be good, or whether it be evil."*

If you are a born again Christian; we like to encourage you in your Christian life. If you are not a born again Christian we can help you here receive genuine salvation.

"Therefore if any man be in Christ, he is a new creature: old things are passed away; behold, all things are become new." **2cor5:17**

What must I do to determine my divine visitation?

To determine divine visitation you must be born again. The word says as many as received him, to them gave He power to become the sons of God. Even to them that believe on his name.

To qualify for divine visitation do the following sincerely,

1) Acknowledge that you are a sinner and that He died for you. **Rom3:23**.

2) Repent of your sins. **Acts 3:19, Luke13:5, 2Peter3:9**

3) Believe in your heart that Jesus died for your sin. **Romans10:10**

4) Confess Jesus as the Lord over your life. **Romans10:10, Acts2:2**

Chapter 2 - What are Hinrances to Prayer

Now repeat this Prayer after me

Say Lord Jesus, I accept you today, as my Lord and my savior, forgive me of my sins wash me with your blood. Right now, I believe, I am sanctified, I am save, I am free, I am free from the Power of sin to serve the Lord Jesus. Thank you Lord for saving me. Amen.

WISDOM KEYS

Every Productive Society is a society heading to the top

Millions of Nigerians run away from Nigeria, very few Nigerians stay in Nigeria.

My decision to return Nigeria is the will of God for my life

My short coming in America after 18 years, trained me to be wise, to think, reflect and reason appropriately.

If you train your mind to reason it will train your hands to earn money.

It is absurd to use the money of the heathen to build the kingdom of the living God.

Every Ministry reveals its agenda and goal either at the beginning or at the end. Be careful of your life it is your first Ministry.

The average American mind is conditioned for a continual quest to get new things and (discard the former) and throw away old things.

Chapter 2 - What are Hinrances to Prayer

When I considered well, my BMW jeep became my initial deposit for the work of the ministry in Nigeria

Everyone is waiting for you to change your mind until you change your thinking nothing changes around you.

Multiple academic degrees in other discipline gave me the chance to think, reflect and reason

What so everyone are thinking and reflecting at the moment reveals you to the time and the now factor

All events and intents are the product of precise thought processes, accurate reason every event is designed for a designated timeline

Wisdom is your ability to think, to create and invent. If you can think wise enough you will come out of penury

The distance between you and success is your creative ability to think reason and reflect accurate.

Success is the result of hard work, commitment resolve and determination learning from past mistakes and failing.

If you organize your mind you have organized your life and destiny.

There is a thin line between success and failure. If you look above and beyond you are on your way to success.

Wealth is your ability to think, power is your ability to reason and success is your ability to be informed.

If you can make use of your mind by thinking and reasoning God will make use of your life and destiny.

Think and Be Great

Reflect, Reason, think and be great

Famous people are born of woman

Chapter 2 - What are Hinrances to Prayer

That you will make it is your intention; that you will survive is your resolve, that you will succeed with changes is your determination, personal efforts and hard work.

No man was born a failure. Lack of vision is the end product of failure.

Working with mental patients encourages and aspire me to be a productive observant and dedicated to my assignment.

Successful people are not magicians, it is the will power combined with hard work, and determination and a resolve to succeed that make them succeed.

In the unequivocal state of the mind, intention is not a location or a position it is the state of the mind.

So many people think that they think. The mind is used to think reflect and reason. You will remain blind with your eye open until you can see with your mind by thinking.

There is no favoritism in accurate and precise calculation

Although knowledge is power, information is the key and gateway to a great future.

It will take the hand of God to move the hand of man.

With the backing of the great wise God, nothing will disconnect you from your inheritance.

As long as you have wisdom and understanding of God, Satan and evil cannot manipulate your life and destiny.

You have come this far by yourself judgment and decision you have made in the past, now lean and listen to God for another dimension of greatness.

Great people are common people it is extra ordinary effort and the price of sacrifice that produces greatness.

As a mental direct care worker I saw a great pastor and a motivational speaker within myself.

Menial job does not reduce your self-worth, until you resolve to achieve greatness see greatness in all you do; you will never count in your community

Chapter 2 - What are Hinrances to Prayer

The principle of Jesus will solve your gambling and addiction problems

The man of Jesus will lead you into heaven,

Everyone have their self-appraisal and what they think about you. Until you discover yourself other opinion about you will alter the real you.

Supervisors and directors are just a position in the chain of command in a work place. Never allow your supervisor hierarchy to alter your opinion about yourself.

Everyone can come out of debt if they make up their mind.

That I am not a decision maker at work does not diminish my contribution to my world.

Although it appears like it was a poor decision to accept a direct care employment at a psychiatric hospital as I reflect of my nine years of experience, it became apparent that I have learnt and experienced enough for my next assignment.

Self-encouragement and determination is a resolve of the heart.

If you are determined to make a difference, and do the things that make a difference you will eventually make a difference.

Good things do not come easy

Short cuts will cut your life short.

Those who look ahead move ahead.

Life is all about making an impact. In your life time strive to make an impact in your community.

Make friends and connect with people who are moving ahead of you in life.

If you can look around well you have come a long way in your life, made a lot of difference and realized a lot of success in life.

If you are my old friend, hurry up to reach out to me before I become a stranger to you.

Everything I am blessed with inspirations from God, that change my definition and interpretation of the world around me.

I thought I was stagnant and lonely until I looked around and noticed my children running around and my wife cooking.

Chapter 2 - What are Hinrances to Prayer

At 40 I resigned my Job to seek the Lord forever.

My ministry took a drastic rise to the top when the wisdom of God visited me with knowledge and understanding.

You will be a better person if you understand the characteristics of your personality – your mood swings attitudes and habits.

It is the seed of love you sow into the heart of a child and a woman that you reap in due time.

Love is not selfish, love share everything including the concealed secrets of the mind.

As long as you have a prayer life and a bible; you will never feel lonely, rejected and idle in the race of life.

When good friends disconnect from you, let them go, they might have seen something new in a different direction.

Confidence in yourself and in God is the only way to bring you out of captivity

Never train a child to waste his/her time.

The mind is the greatest assets of a great future.

You walk by common sense run by principles and fly by instruction.

Those who fly in flight of life fly alone.

Up in the air you are alone. No one can toll you accept the compass of knowledge and information

I have seen a tolling vehicle I have seen a tolling ship I have never seen a tolling airplane.

I exercise my judgment and make a decision every minute of the day.

Decisions are crucial, critical and vital with reference to your future.

So many people wish for a great future. You can only work towards a great future.

Your celebrity status began when you discovered your talent. What are you good at? Work at it with all commitment.

Prayers will sustain you but the wisdom of God will prosper you.

When I met Oyedepo, his teachings changed my perspective, but when I met Ibiyeomie; His teaching changed my perception.

I will be successful in ministry if only I concentrate and focus my energy in the work of the ministry.

It took the late Dr. Vincent Pearle Norman's book to open my mind towards kingdom success.

CHAPTER 3

PRAYER OF SALVATION

"Neither is there salvation in any other: for there is none other name under heaven given among men, whereby we must be saved." **Acts4:12.**

What must I do to determine my salvation?

To be saved we must be born again! The word says as many as received him, to them gave He power to become the sons of God. Even to them that believe on his name.

To qualify for divine visitation do the following sincerely,

1) Acknowledge that you are a sinner and that He died for you. **Rom3:23.**

2) Repent of your sins. **Acts 3:19, Luke13:5, 2Peter3:9**

3) Believe in your heart that Jesus died for your sin. **Romans10:10**

4) Confess Jesus as the Lord over your life. **Romans10:10, Acts2:21**

Now repeat this Prayer after me

Say Lord Jesus, I accept you today, as my Lord and my savior, forgive me of my sins wash me with your blood. Right now, I believe, I am sanctified, I am save, I am free, I am free from the Power of sin to serve the Lord Jesus. Thank you Lord for saving me. Amen.

I adjure you to watch the Spirit of God bear witness with your Spirit confirming His word with signs following. The word says The Spirit itself beareth witness with our spirit, that we are the children of God.

Chapter 3 - Prayer of Salvation

MIRACLE CARE OUTREACH

"...But that the members should have the same care one for another" **1cor12:25**

We are all members of the body of Christ. Jesus commanded us to love our neighbor as ourselves. This includes caring for one another as a member of one body. True love is expressed in caring and giving. The word says for God so Love He gave....

Reach out to someone in need of Jesus, help someone in crisis find Christ. Look out and prove your love to Jesus by caring and inviting your friends and associates to find Jesus the Healer.

Invite your friends to our Home Care Cell Fellowship (Miracle chapel Intl Satellite fellowship) In the USA at 33 Schley Street Newark New Jersey 07112.

If you are in Nigeria—**MIRACLE OF GOD MINISTRIES**

A.K.A"MIRACLE CHAPEL INTL" Mpama –Egbu-Owerri Imo state Nigeria.

(Home Care Cell fellowship Group). We meet every Tuesday at 6:00pm-7:00pm.

LIFE IS NOT ALL ABOUT DURATION BUT ITS ALL ABOUT DONATION

What does the above statement mean?....

"Life consists not in accumulation of material wealth.." **Luke12:15.**

"But it's all about liberality....meaning- what you can give and share with others." **Proverb11:25.**

When you live for others--You live forever- because you out live your generation by the legacy you live behind after you depart into glory to be with the Lord. But when you live to yourself - you are reduced to self—you are easily forgotten when you die and depart in glory.

Permit me to admonish you today to live your life to be a blessing to a soul connected to you today.

Chapter 3 - Prayer of Salvation

I want you to know that so many souls are connected and looking up to you, and through you so many souls will be saved and rescued from destruction. Will you disciple someone today to find Jesus Christ?

"As a genuine Christian; it is your duty to evangelize Jesus Christ to all you meet on your way. Jesus is still in the healing business-Jesus is still doing miracles from time of old to now.

Therefore tell someone about Jesus Christ today, disciple and bring them to Church."

John 1:45 Philip findeth Nathanael....

Please to prove the sincerity of your love for God today; please become a soul winner. The dignity of your Christianity is hidden in your boldness to proclaim and evangelize Jesus Christ to all you meet on your way.

There is a question mark on the integrity of your Christianity until you become a life soul winner. Invite someone to join us worship the Lord Jesus this coming Sunday.

MIRACLE OF GOD MINISTRIES

PILLARS OF THE COMMISSION

We Believe Preach and Practice the following,

1) We believe and preach Salvation to every living human being

2) We believe and preach Repentance and forgiveness of sins

3) We believe and preach the baptism of the Holy Spirit and Spiritual gifts

4) We believe and teach the Prosperity

5) We believe and preach Divine Healing and Miracles (Signs &Wonder)

6) We believe and preach Faith

7) We believe and Proclaim the Power of God (Supernatural)

8) We believe and Proclaim Praise& Worship to God

Chapter 3 - Prayer of Salvation

9) We believe and preach Wisdom

10) We believe and preach Holiness (Consecration)

11) We believe and preach Vision

12) We believe and teach the Word of God

13) We believe and teach Success

14) We believe and practice Prayer

15) We believe and teach Deliverance

This 15 stones form the Pillars of Our Commission.

Become part of this church family and follow this great move of God.

MY HEART FELT PRAYER FOR YOU

It is my prayer that you testify today about the goodness of the Lord. I desire for you to have an encounter with our Lord Jesus Christ.

Now let me Pray for you:

Heavenly father may today be a day of new beginning for this precious love one. Lord God of heaven open a new chapter in the life of this precious love one reading this book today. May all their prayers be answered in the mighty name of Jesus. We thank you Jesus for hearing us. In Jesus mighty name. Amen.

Chapter 3 - Prayer of Salvation

WHAT TO DO WHEN MIRACLE SEEMS TO BE DELAYED:

1. Praise God even in times of trouble, trial, and tribulations.

2. Be expectant- expect God to move beyond imagination.

3) Be willing and Obedient-God look at your obedient in times of delay.

4) Be focus—God expect us to pay relevant attention to details.

5) Do not quit- If we must emerge winners, quitting is not an option.

6) Be positive—it can only get better so be positive.

7) Be optimistic--- Your case is different so be optimistic in life.

8) Develop all possibility mentality—Every limitation is within you faith.

CHAPTER 4
ABOUT THE AUTHOR

Rev Franklin N Abazie is the founding and Presiding Pastor of Miracle of God Ministries with headquarters in Newark, New Jersey USA and a branch church in Owerri- Imo State Nigeria. He is following the footsteps of one of his mentors, Oral Roberts (Healing Evangelist) of the blessed memory.

The Lord passed Oral Roberts healing mantle two days before he went to be with the Lord at age 91 into the hand of healing evangelist-Rev Franklin N Abazie in a vision.

In all his services the Power and Presence of God is present to heal all in his audience. He is an ordained man of God with a Healing Ministry reviving the healing and miracle ministry of Jesus Christ of Nazareth.

Chapter 4 - About the Author

Pastor Franklin N Abazie, is called by God with a unique mandate:

"THE MOMENT IS DUE TO IMPACT YOUR WORLD THROUGH THE REVIVAL OF THE HEALING & MIRACLE MINISTRY OF JESUS CHRIST OF NAZARETH.

I AM SENDING YOU TO RESTORE HEALTH UNTO THEE AND I WILL HEAL THEE OF THY WOUNDS. SAID THE LORD OF HOST"

He is a gifted ardent Teacher of the word of God who operates also in the office of a Prophet, generating and attracting undeniable signs & wonders, special miracles and healings, with apostolic fireworks of the Holy Ghost.

He is the founding and presiding senior Pastor of this fast growing Healing ministry.

He has written over 86 inspirational, healing and transforming books covering almost all aspect of divine healing and life. He is happily married and blessed with children.

BOOKS BY REV FRANKLIN N ABAZIE

1) Commanding Abundance
2) The outcome of faith
3) Understanding the secret of prevailing prayers
4) Understanding the secret of the man God uses
5) Activating my due Season
6) Overcoming Divine Verdicts
7) The Outcome of Divine Wisdom
8) Understanding God's Restoration Mandate
9) Walking in the Victory and Authority of the truth
10) Gods Covenant Exemption
11) Destiny Restoration Pillars
12) Provoking Acceptable Praise
13) Understanding Divine Judgment
14) Activating Angelic Re-enforcement
15) Provoking Un-Merited Favor
16) The Benefits of the Speaking faith
17) Understanding Divine Arrangement

18) Understanding Divine Healing
19) The Mystery of Endurance
20) Obeying Divine Instructions
21) Understanding the Voice of God
22) Never give up on Hope
23) The prevailing Power of faith
24) Understanding Divine Prosperity
25) The Reward of Prayer
26) Covenant Keys to Answered Prayers
27) Activating the Forces of Vengeance
28) Put your faith to work
29) Where is your trust?
30) The Audacity of the Blood of Jesus
31) Redeeming Your Days
32) The force of Vision
33) Breaking the shackles of Family Curses
34) Wisdom for Marriage Stability
35) Overcoming prevailing challenges
36) The Prayer solution
37) The power of Prayer
38) The Effective Strategy of Prayer
39) The prayer that works
40) Walking in Forgiveness
41) The power of the grace of God

42) The Power of Persistence
43) Overcoming Divine verdicts
44) The audacity of the blood of Jesus.
45) The prevailing power of the blood of Jesus
46) The benefit of the speaking faith.
47) Fearless faith
48) Redeeming Your Days.
49) The Supernatural Power of Prophecy
50) The companionship of the Holy Spirit
51) Understanding Divine Judgement
52) Understanding Divine Prosperity
53) Dominating Controlling Forces
54) The winners Faith
55) Destiny Restoration Pillars
56) Developing Spiritual Muscles
57) Inexplicable faith
58) The lifestyle of Prayer
59) Developing a positive attitude in life.
60) The mystery of Divine supply
61) Encounter with the Power of God
62) Walking in love
63) Praying in the Spirit
64) How to provoke your testimony

65) Walking in the reality of the Anointing
66) The reality of new birth
67) The price of freedom
68) The Supernatural power of faith
69) The intellectual components of Redemption
70) Overcoming Fear
71) Overcoming Prevailing Challenges
72) My life & Ministry
73) The Mystery of Praise

MIRACLE OF GOD MINISTRIES

NIGERIA CRUSADE 2012

MIRACLE OF GOD MINISTRIES
NIGERIA CRUSADE 2012

MIRACLE OF GOD MINISTRIES

NIGERIA CRUSADE

2012

MIRACLE OF GOD MINISTRIES

NIGERIA CRUSADE

2012

www.ingramcontent.com/pod-product-compliance
Lightning Source LLC
Chambersburg PA
CBHW021441080526
44588CB00009B/637